BIJOUX IN THE DARK

LETTER MACHINE EDITIONS   TUCSON, AZ   SEATTLE, WA

BIJOUX IN THE DARK

John Yau

Also by John Yau

Poetry

Crossing Canal Street (1975)

The Reading of an Ever-Changing Tale (1977)

Sometimes (1979)

Broken Off by the Music (1981)

Corpse and Mirror (1983)

Radiant Silhouette: New & Selected Work 1974-1988 (1989)

Big City Primer (1991), with photographs by Bill Barrette

Edificio Sayonara (1992)

Berlin Diptychon (1995), with photographs by Bill Barrette

Forbidden Entries (1996)

I Was a Poet in the House of Frankenstein (2000)

Borrowed Love Poems (2002)

Ing Grish (2005), with Thomas Nozkowski

Paradiso Diaspora (2006)

Exhibits (2010)

Further Adventures in Monochrome (2012)

Egyptian Sonnets (2012)

Fiction

The Sleepless Night of Eugene Delacroix (1980)

Hawaiian Cowboys (1995)

My Symptoms (1996)

My Heart Is That Eternal Rose Tattoo (2001)

Criticism

The Passionate Spectator: Essays on Art and Poetry (2006)

The Wild Children of William Blake (2017)

Collaborations

100 More Jokes from the Book of the Dead (2001), with Archie Rand

Monographs

In The Realm of Appearances: The Art of Andy Warhol (1993)
A. R. Penck (1993)
Ed Moses: A Retrospective of Paintings and Drawings, 1951 – 1996 (1996)
The United States of Jasper Johns (1996)
Joan Mitchell: Works on Paper 1956 – 1992 (2007)
A Thing Among Things: The Art of Jasper Johns (2008)
William Tillyer: Watercolours (2010)
Jay DeFeo: Chiaroscuro (2013)
Mernet Larsen (2013)
Sam Francis (2014)
Richard Artschwager: Into the Desert (2015)
Catherine Murphy (2016)
Al Taylor: Early Paintings (2017)
Thomas Nozkowski (2017)
Philip Taaffe (2018)

Editor

The Collected Poems of Fairfield Porter (1985), with David Kermani
Fetish (1998)

Published by Letter Machine Editions
Tucson, Arizona
Seattle, Washington
© 2018 by John Yau
Cover image: Untitled (M-63), 2016. © Thomas Nozkowski, courtesy Pace Gallery
All Rights Reserved
Book Design by HR Hegnauer
Printed in Canada
Cataloging-in-Publication Data is on file at the Library of Congress

ISBN: 978-0-9887137-8-9

lettermachine.org

Distributed to the trade by Small Press Distribution (spdbooks.org)

Table of Contents

Preamble
3 Hearsay Song

I. Blacke Calender
7   Fortunes, Favorite Sayings, and Assorted Sundries from a *Blacke Calender*
10 Descriptions, Illuminations, and Assorted Sundries from a *Blacke Calender*
14 A Painter's Formulas, An Alchemist's Notes, and an Unknown Convict's Ravings found on a *Blacke Calender*
17 Ravings from a *Blacke Calender*

II.
21 Music from Childhood
22 Portrait
23 The Poet
24 The Blackest Black Forest
25 Playtime
26 Moth-Eaten Tapestry with Cigarette Burns
27 First Language Lesson
28 After I Turned Sixty-Five
29 I Dreamed The Senator Announced on National Television
31 Inauguration Day
32 The New Colossus as Donald Trump
33 O Pinyin Sonnet (1)
34 O Pinyin Sonnet (2)
35 O Pinyin Sonnet (3)
36 O Pinyin Sonnet (4)
37 O Pinyin Sonnet (5)
38 O Pinyin Sonnet (6)

39	O Pinyin Sonnet (7)
40	O Pinyin Sonnet (8)
41	O Pinyin Sonnet (9)
42	I Heard A Man Say
44	Something To Look Forward To
45	News Item
46	Dante's Carousel
47	Barnum and Bosch (1)
48	Barnum and Bosch (2)
49	Pan's Tomb

III. Firefly Promises

53	After an Anonymous Student of Albrecht Durer and Hieronymus Bosch
54	Written in the Shadow of Francis Bacon's *Self-Portrait Triptych* (1985-86)
56	Written in the Shadows Cast by *The Burning of the Houses of Lords and Commons* (1835) by J. M. W Turner
59	At the Tomb of Narcissus
60	Firefly Promises
65	Black Threads from Meng Chiao (1)
67	Black Threads from Meng Chiao (2)
70	Black Threads from Meng Chiao (3)
73	The Detective's Love Letter

IV. Egyptian Sonnets

77	Egyptian Sonnets 1 - 22

V. *Bijoux in the Dark*

101	Biopic
103	Movie Night
104	Shipboard Entertainment
106	Ten Successful Adventure Movie Formulas

107	Ten Famous Outtakes
108	Ten Enduring Statements from Lost or Forgotten Films
109	Bijoux in the Dark
111	Film Reviewer

VI.

115	Other Local Delights
116	Different Drum
122	Overnight
123	Standard Operating Procedure
124	Three, Not Four Seasons
125	Advice to the Love Worn
127	Angry Birds

Coda

131	Midway

For Eve and Cerise

PREAMBLE

Hearsay Song

They are dying out and I want to reach them before they are gone
Not that I know what I would say to them when I get there
Their songs rippling beneath temporary sky
As I approach, as I am doing now
Even though I am nowhere near wherever they are
Swirling in blossoming dust and dreaming they are not

They are dying out and I want to reach them before they are gone
Just as I want to reach myself before I too am gone
Another blossom sliding into slime
What notes do I hear drenched in fiery sky
Are these ghosts rising up before me
Or gasps of dust near a lake covered by algae

They are dying out and I want to reach them before their names vanish
Before they become ghosts dying in pink algae and ruined vowels
Not that I know what their songs say
Telling sting of monstrous human torrent
Wheeling above burning story of lost lives
Tapering branches of smoke, red and yellow leaves falling

They are dying out and I want to reach them
Before my name joins theirs in plastic matrimony
Before a blue-eyed undertaker powders my nose
Or I turn to powder in squirt gun of unprofitable insects
Secrets folded away never rinsed in scum corner
History erasing traces of its nothing new

I.
Blacke Calender

Fortunes, Favorite Sayings, and Assorted Sundries from a *Blacke Calender*

1.
Dust drifts across elliptical sky.

2.
This is my biography. It tells the story of someone I never met.

3.
This bayonet star is key ring swirl in renewable cup, night's unwinding bowl, silvery drops licked off dead stars for bullion and gumption, juice injected into a journey undertaken long ago, before you were deposited on a forsaken rock, another cloud of questions stirring air's blackened shadows.

4.
You hear yourself talking and walking toward precincts of sky that remain closed to you, having banished you, staining the ovals of black and amber air again, as you sally forth from kingdom of craven knaves, dismal whiffs scudding across ceiling, doors banging in the wind.

What are you saying, you say to yourself.

Where will this talking take you?

5.
Once a voice leaves a room, it cannot be caught.

6.
Stop for a moment's quivering and think: what does breathing steal from you with each breath? Are you any more than a debilitating sequence walking down a posh street in collapsed underwear, always dependably expendable, poor imitations of a silent scream passing through your illuminated skin and inked parchment?

A sign in a window: What is the poet's place on the totem of the tribe?

Is this the question you return to? Or is it the one you leave, its silhouette etched into non-reflective glass?

7.
There is no way you can cross the border with confiscated photographs locked inside your head — glossy drifts behind rheumy eyes. The body is a spitting stump that defecates by side of road, an added passage, an acrostic that does not add up, ghost of listening to antique dead rewrite a dream inviting you back to life, its daily carnage delivered in upturned caps.

Please adjust this channel in the future, which shivers at your approach.

8.
How has your capacity for sympathetic murmurs extended your coexistence quotient?

Have you dialed into a member of a crying species yet? Or have you put that encounter on hold?

Have you locked your horns of plenty so that no music is lost?

How can you spare time when your shopping cart is full?

9.
You hear a voice behind you say: The promise was not made, nor was it kept.

10.
When nothing you wear moves you closer to heaven's boat, time flies into the wind and does not return, a bird with a note pinned to its burlap throat.

11.
In the dream, you file proper documents, leave dulled body behind. Thrill moves you up the chain, turns water into swine, the kind you eat only when your mouth is full of tiny wings.

12.
What will you do with this pile of broken boxes, these dried flowers, this shoe nailed to the wall? I will live in them until they split apart.

13.
The mirror is an oval, an empty eye. The rain finds you crouched in a corner, singing songs you never heard until now, old songs, they must have been waiting for you to fetch them from the sky.

The shadow of a passing bird stays printed on your face and hands.

14.
One of us lives on a street known for its buckets of glass eyes, bad tunes to fill in the black holes when daylight absconds with the conversation between us suspended until further notice.

15.
The light coming from the stars is full of death.

16.
The bird looks in the mirror and falls asleep.

Descriptions, Illuminations, and Assorted Sundries from a *Blacke Calender*

1.
Moonlight's ink fills this empty song.

2.
For the time being, words of comfort have been put aside.

3.
Unstable and seditious weather.

4.
Guide to remnants of last known sublunary investigation platform.

5.
Street of Abandoned Accomplices
Alleyway of False Denominators
Plaza of Snake Stranglers
Arch of Ossification
Dungeon of Ancient Cosmologies

6.
The city is currently a faulty immune system, a porous fortification protected by the smile of Medusa, and many of its copies; ghosts of enlightened Pharoahs; collections of bird agendas; armed intellectual convicts and their difficult converts; and fleets of renovated submarines — a telecommunications network along which your particles pass.

7.
Do not approach it in the mirror you hold before you.

8.
Filching is a compulsion that requires immediate attention.

9.
The city is an amphitheater of egos, a semi-enclosed form where massacres can be found on the daily menu.

10.
Renters are condemned to sit on stones.

11.
Signs of Uncontrollable Twitch Factor: the ghosts of commodities
penetrate every known protection until they turn into desirable maxims.

12.
The Fascination Business and the Eagerness to Witness Failure

13.
Circles no longer offer immunity.

14.
Morning's streaked stems dissolve before reaching the city's last row of windows, their blinking sovereignty.

15.
Orb distractors are wired for secondary sounds, any sign of toxic self-ventilation that interrupts the motivation to obtain.

16.
These ocean fires, which periodically open up along the border, where opposing representations take precedence, must not be tampered with: this information frenzy is to be gained without succumbing to messianic affirmation.

17.
Nothing can throw off the flames of frenzy once they attain critical momentum, a fullness that is secured by a swarm of radiant messengers turning themselves into more than themselves.

18.
This is the opposite of the habitus of the renter moving back and forth between gloomy domicile and cheerful cubbyhole.

19.
Heroes are not cards to search for in an arranged pile.

20.
The permanent agency that you are looking for has either been moved or no longer exists. Please consult the nearest directory.

21.
Please ignore the next artificial proclamation.

22.

Consider the latest discharge from a dazzled witness: the plant kingdom's idea of burial has become itchy and intolerable.

23.

Melodies change in an inferno, where proportion is eliminated by signals sent from a distant star.

24.

Expenditure is followed by escalation, the commercial transformation and distribution of language's scream.

25.

Just because your head is held aloft, as a substitute lantern, does not mean light is forthcoming.

A Painter's Formulas, An Alchemist's Notes, and an Unknown Convict's Ravings found on a *Blacke Calender*

1.
I could not have written these words until I played the game of second-guessing.

2.
Every word is a stab in the dark, a treatise about a parallel condition.

3.
Poetry is another way of writing in sand.

4.
This inscription was chiseled onto the marble base:

You must be able to change into the wind or a leafless tree in a parking lot.
You must recognize that you can never attain these states of fruitfulness.

5.
Words are synonyms and swords are letters.

6.
Play the field
Flay the peeled

7.
What happens when words (or sounds) become colors, and a thunderclap descends into swirls of red?

8.
You will be guided by one sign: The fish does not know it lives in the sea.

9.
It all starts with Red, Yellow, and Blue.

10.
Certain tints of Brown and Violet are derived from the ground-up remains of ancient Egyptian felines mixed with white pitch, myrrh, and bitumen.

11.
These words were written on the wall of an empty storehouse:

There is a candle that was forsaken until its flame turned to gold.
There is a room in which blue cadavers are washed with warm milk.
There is a field that pulses whenever clouds block out the sun.

12.
The blue and rose stamp is of the face of a young boy, perhaps a prince who never left adolescence behind. A pressed circle of wax buries his mouth beneath a fleshy red moon or, as some younger scholars claim, seals his lips with the determined vengeance of infinity.

13.
The originals are known only through the descriptions passed down to us, written on the skins of extinct animals, the actual objects having been heaved up into clouds of startled excitement by those fleeing the pestilence.

14.
The dirt must be pounded gently before it is sifted through a sieve woven from the hairs of a horse's tail.

15.
Despite the distances between them, the heads are all perfectly aligned, as if strung on a stretched clothesline.

16.
A sword needs only one tooth.

17.
The problem with description is that it makes a bad copy.

18.
Tragedy's mask has not been torn away.

19.
A nail was used to scratch the word "cemetery" into a painting of the ocean. A tiny brush added a stream of gray tears falling from one of the stars.

Ravings from a *Blacke Calender*

1.
Better to put a safety pin through your lips than a nail in your right eye.

2.
Better to stamp on your ancestor's grave than be stopped in your neighbor's yard.

3.
I made a glyph for the brain when it's on fire.

4.
I copy down the sounds I hear inside my head,
the perfect copy I carry under my arm
when I want people to stay away.

5.
I turn on the radio and dance to commercials.
I love to hum happy jingles written by unemployed undertakers.
I want them to know that their last breath can be a song
landing softly in outstretched hands.

6.
I keep my mustache in a pocket that I have sewn shut.

7.
I want to learn how to sell lingo and leather straps

8.
I have been folded into this: a paper version of a drunken boat
crisscrossing the sea without a rudder.

I sit in a bathtub fashioned from polished white bones.

Men painted blue and men wearing fuzzy red pajamas,
devils with tails and horns, pelted me with words.

Those who tell you words are not sticks and stones are lying.

9.
I wash my face with sand. I pour water onto the ashes
and use the ink to write my name. I draw an outline of a cloud.

10.
I live inside this furniture, my eyes pointed toward the stars,
black dots bristling in the sky.

11.
Give me your glass of tears and the gunfire you hear each time you open your eyes.

II.

Music from Childhood

You grow up hearing two languages. Neither fits your fits
Your mother informs you "moon" means "window to another world"

You begin to hear words mourn the sounds buried inside their mouths
A row of yellow windows and a painting of them

Your mother informs you "moon" means "window to another world"
You decide it is better to step back and sit in the shadows

A row of yellow windows and a painting of them
Someone said you can see a blue pagoda or a red rocket ship

You decide it is better to step back and sit in the shadows
Is it because you saw a black asteroid fly past your window

Someone said you can see a blue pagoda or a red rocket ship
I tried to follow in your footsteps, but they turned to water

Is it because I saw a black asteroid fly past my window
The air hums — a circus performer riding a bicycle towards the ceiling

I tried to follow in your footsteps, but they turned to water
The town has started sinking back into its commercial

The air hums — a circus performer riding a bicycle towards the ceiling
You grow up hearing two languages. Neither fits your fits

The town has started sinking back into its commercial
You begin to hear words mourn the sounds buried inside their mouths

Portrait

Or is it
a poor trait

I am a parasite
I lift off

the wings of others

The Poet

after Peter Rühmkorf

Your fingers fit so beautifully into my wounds
I become wavering lines of dotted notes

Tremolo strung up beneath paper sky
I bite words in half, lick blood, and sigh

My wit consists of spots on my skin
deposited there by your brief happiness

before departing for other side of Paradise
a word that children are forbidden to use

unless it is right before they climb the ladder
to the infinite heaven of their cold bed

Your fingers fit so beautifully into my wounds
I dance to pitter-patter tears and music's cozy fire

The Blackest Black Forest

Just *nada y nada*, which means drop dead in your cleanest socks, o grand and fearless pumpkin. Whether brave or bedraggled or both, the fact that you can put anything (or anyone) into my poem doesn't mean that you should submit an innocent biped to the vagaries of an adventure, escapade, or journey, any exploit that might be considered a quest, search, mission, or hunt. Haven't you been listening? Don't you press your ears to the airwaves? Undertakings in which there is something momentous, earth shattering, or life changing waiting at an undisclosed location (the end) have not (repeat) been acceptable, or even advisable, for decades (insert longer time frame). It is nostalgia personified ever since (ever since) the price of gasoline began rising, the increased industrial capacity of our treacherous neighbors to the east became an economic factor, and the calamitous aftermath of the fall of grandiose empires to the north and south. Officially speaking, there are to be no further missions, pursuits, or expeditions, either within the domain of this poem or outside its porous borders, in the no-man's land of ruined kingdoms, broken oil derricks and growing silt deposits. Any such chase could, would, and should end in disaster, an upsetting of the lately achieved balance, a crisis that is to be avoided now that villagers across the land have erected new traffic signals outside their municipal swimming pools. Listen to what they are saying — Please be careful when approaching the crosswalk; and be advised that the starlings, nuthatches, and finches must be collectively recognized for their contributions to the recent paper drive. This is the poem in which you are most happy, the one that most closely resembles you in all your minor notes of glory.

Playtime

Time for this infomercial to be over and the next era to begin
Like other aspiring tots, you grew up and quickly became outdated

Is there a place in the sediment reserved for those stuck in your price range
I have tried to be reasonable, but your actions are that of a churlish comet

Like other aspiring tots, you grew up and quickly became outdated
Try the cleansing soap, it will give you another sudsy soporific to latch onto

I have tried to be reasonable, but your actions are that of a churlish comet
Do you really think the scribes can't copy down the stars' curlicue route

Try the cleansing soap, it will give you another sudsy soporific to latch onto
Being an acrobat isn't just dubious, it's an assault on gravity

Do you really think the scribes can't copy down the stars' curlicue route
Flagrant violation is when I tell you reality TV is better than the real thing

Being an acrobat isn't just dubious, it's an assault on gravity
What do you think I am, your latest mental health sidekick

Flagrant violation is when I tell you reality TV is better than the real thing
Let's go down to cafeteria and poke our fingers in the vanilla pudding

What do you think I am, your latest mental health sidekick
Time for this infomercial to be over and the next era to begin

Let's go down to cafeteria and poke our fingers in the vanilla pudding
Is there a place in the sediment reserved for those stuck in your price range

Moth-Eaten Tapestry with Cigarette Burns

Welcome to the latest, unedited edition.

Inside a tunnel of the centrally located railway station and department store, two dogs argue over the contents of a nearby garbage dump. The first dog is an import from China, which he claims is irrefutable proof of the innate superiority of his gene pool stretching back to the plains of nutrient rich, yellow earth. The other dog, which isn't a native of these parts and doesn't rightly know where he came from, disagrees, but can go no further with his argument, which causes him to feel intense shame for not possessing the terminology that would enable him to verbally rip apart the first dog's head, where his intellect supposedly resides. So begins a larger quarrel that has been annexing surrounding hills and meandering riverbeds right up to this day, the one that you are standing in, feet firmly planted in the mutilated earth, blue mud up to your knees.

The problem of survival in extreme conditions is a perennial predicament, which we, as poor practitioners of a lost art, have never fully addressed, preferring any means of deferral possible, including false advertising. This is our legacy. If the moon's ascendancy is a barometer of the possible achievements that lie in wait just around the next bend, then it is time to get this boat in the water. Once you are floating downstream or paddling upstream, pause and take notice of the grayest stars, as they are capable of guiding you to the outskirts of a town that will soon be flooded with all manner of detritus, which you might find to your liking — mackinaws, microphones, and machetes. From there, you must make your way to a jewelry store that has flourished in a neighborhood that few residents have ever left, satisfied that every alarm they hear is false.

The first of the outer vestibules is likely to be quite cool, as the transition is crucial to your continued health. You will find the waiting room to your liking. Please relax in any chair that embraces you with dignity and enjoy the remains of your chocolate ice cream palace. Remember that all requests must be limited to twenty-four characters or less, with or without spaces.

First Language Lesson

As you may have inferred, Ka Pow is not a spicy chicken dish
Meanwhile, you are an accident waiting to repurpose yourself

Who are you to mix up languages? This is not a smorgasbord
You have to remember that you are a cylinder, a form of fodder

Meanwhile, you are an accident waiting to repurpose yourself
Why do you need an expensive phone? It won't help you in the future

You have to remember that you are a cylinder, a form of fodder
Our company motto: other than you, no waste shall go to waste

Why do you need an expensive phone? It won't help you in the future
Have you ever thought of joining the circus? You might find a home there

Our company motto: other than you, no waste shall go to waste
Choosing suitable punishments is an unavoidable necessity

Have you ever thought of joining the circus? You might find a home there.
If you are speaking about my place in the universe, that's not right

Choosing suitable punishments is an unavoidable necessity
Hasn't the sky repeatedly proven to be the most excellent manager

If you are speaking about my place in the universe, that's not right
Memories are iridescent insects infiltrating your dreams

Hasn't the sky repeatedly proven to be the most excellent manager
Little sphinxes, I have instructed you to the best of my ability

Memories are iridescent insects infiltrating your dreams
As you may have inferred, Ka Pow is not a spicy chicken dish

Little sphinxes, I have instructed you to the best of my ability
Who are you to mix up languages? This is not a smorgasbord

After I Turned Sixty-Five

I start asking my co-workers if any of them want to rub my invisible tattoos
I tell neighbors to ponder clarity as if it is something that can be grasped
I pretend to be an insubordinate squirrel at family gatherings
I memorize how to be vile in different languages
I take up designer drugs and change my taste in music
I secretly keep track of all the people who call me "Pops"
I burn down my childhood tenement in a gentle fashion
I try different styles and flavors and announce that none of them suit me
I call a halt to all relationships that smack of the personal
I babble whenever someone asks me for directions
I tell lies about my adolescence in order to impress strangers with my pain
I learn to make the sounds of a man who is happily surprised
I insulate myself with voice mail and incompetence

I Dreamed The Senator Announced on National Television

If you are over sixty-five you should do us all a favor
You should hurry up and die as cheaply and efficiently as possible
This being America
These are the facts —
You're a drag on society
A stick stuck in the wheel of progress
I don't why we still accord you human status
When all you do is take up space and cost us money
Like a bawling infant or a surly pet
When you are neither
And you're aren't spending or saving enough
To justify your pathetic existence
Or you're spending it on laxatives because you are full of shit
And we already got enough on our hands so go on and get out

If you are over sixty-five you need too much attention
And you've already had enough from us and you shouldn't get any more
You whiny bag of flatulence
You slimy patch of expectorant sliding down a dirty wall

If you are over sixty-five the government is sending you money
Wads of money every month because you didn't earn enough
In your lifetime to take care of yourself in your old age
You weren't able to think ahead
Which means you are a failure
As worthless as the trash
My wife carries to the curb every Wednesday morning
Because I am too busy trying to figure out
How to get rid of you and you and you and you
And frankly not a single one of you is worth dealing with

If you are over sixty-five you why not choose cremation
Step into oncoming traffic
Or fall off a bridge
Just get on with it
I am sure there are enough people waiting to pick through
The little heap you accumulated in your miserable life
You might as well end the pain and start giving everything away now
You won't need it where you are going

If you are over sixty-five you are breathing my air
It's time you stop
Because my family and I need it more than you do
We always did

Inauguration Day

If you think the next President
is going to improve your quality of life

you choose to believe
that war is a three-letter word

that does not affect anyone it touches
except the tender pages of youth

You know, those dirty sheets
young lovers write odes on

before they die between blinks

The New Colossus as Donald Trump

after Emma Lazarus

I don't need more tired or poor
Let the mucky masses camp on their own dirty shore
Let them stay wretched, it is what they deserve
Send me only those who know how to bow, scrape, and serve
Or else I will close the gate to my golden hotel

O Pinyin Sonnet (1)

As everyone knows, the Chinese possess
highly sensitive nervous systems:
acute temporary madness following prolonged stress
is episodically endemic among them
(This is why social harmony and peace
and not 'rocking the boat' is paramount
in their societies, wherever they have sprung up)
Fortunately, when they go mad
they generally only harm or kill themselves,
their deranged ire is most often inwardly directed
Their programming is truly different than ours
which explains the multitudinous, hierarchical
non-individualistic (even socially oneiric)
types of societies that exist throughout the Far East
                                    to this day

O Pinyin Sonnet (2)

By the numbers, the Chinese
tend to be pretty good at what they do.
But, in all my years of being their co-worker,
I have learned that they are not
particularly good at much else.
This is why most appear to be happy
little worker bees buzzing around their tasks,
making no ruffles or promotion shuffles
especially if they speak very good English
and, when the occasion calls for it, tell a joke
that is actually funny to those who aren't Chinese.
None of this is entirely their fault.
They grew up differently than the rest of us.
Otherwise I like them and think they are fine.

O Pinyin Sonnet (3)

Though seldom labeled "The Chinaman"
Wong Song, Long Dong or Ding will do.
Still routine to be returned to pulver
in first shockwaves shooting across silver screen
before depth of real story begins.
Bland spotless expression worthy of his race,
usually decked in red, yellow, or highlighter green —
shorthand that he is sacrificial pig
soon to be dangled plunged flushed or frozen
before slurping prognathous blob toting lurkers.
Mildly curious prop destined for smithereen pile.
There must be nothing left to put back together,
not even scraps of scavenged name
much less look-alike face.

O Pinyin Sonnet (4)

Plus I don't understand their food.
Who eats chicken feet and eggs
buried in mud is unwholesome.
Something dirty slithers along
in their uncleanliness you see what
no one is saying is how many of them
like to eat animals that got no eyes
some kind of in-between thing.
Plus what kind of people eat six-
legged creatures and dried duck blood.
You know there is something not right about
putting frogs and grasshoppers together.
They aren't friends on earth — so why
serve them at the same dinner.

O Pinyin Sonnet (5)

I see no reason to let them go on
squawking jibber jabber ching chong
while squatting and squabbling
in pigeon park, acting like it's okay to be here
because you know they bring everyone
even the infirm, and what are they good for,
remember that song,
I used to sing it all the time
before they started sneaking ashore.
Boatloads of them out there in the dark,
waiting to be stacked up, like dried logs,
you can hardly tell the old ones apart,
except maybe by the slant of their crooked teeth.
Doesn't anyone know how to end this broken flood?

O Pinyin Sonnet (6)

Double click me if I am wrong
but they are known to turn bright red
when they imbibe the real stuff
which tells you maybe it's not such a good thing
that they all ride bicycles over there
because the ones here can't drive worth spit.
Maybe it has to do with the tilt of their eyes,
some genetic miscoding that makes them
unfit for the road, just the rage directed
at their squat faces, which I never trusted.
Imagine deliciously repeated pile-ups and benders.
I got nothing against them individually
because as far as I can see
none of them ever quite fit into that category.

O Pinyin Sonnet (7)

I am a history nut blessed
with a third eye when it comes
to hoovering the wormy underside.
Once the floodgates opened
and a thousand businesses bloomed
in the crumbling countryside
we had given the Chinamen a second chance.
So what if I know they helped build the railroad
got blown up by dynamite
and did the laundry.
Is this what my future kids
are going to have to study in school?
When I was young, they were famous
for stealing pigeons from the park.

O Pinyin Sonnet (8)

after Mark Wahlberg

Why bring up that old tirade of slurs
when it was just some slop slipping
from my swollen, drunken tongue?
Me in another life I left behind.
Even as the neighborhood's tarnished star
I can still say that I outshine all of you
but I need not recite that story again
as it's already written in the fat of your lives.
Haven't I learned to be perfectly polite
a form of manipulation none of you
have ever deigned to master?
Don't my donations earn me a second chance?
Some people deserve even more.
Frankly, I am one of them.

O Pinyin Sonnet (9)

after Mark Wahlberg, again

You always and forever got to let everyone know
that you can charm clumps of moolah
into every niche of your empire.
You see, son, I am not just another vanilla magilla.
I had to learn from my messy errors,
rapidly glean how to be a jerk that pleases
the ones who grease wheels and palms.
Yes, I go to church nearly every day,
and I am not so shiny that I won't
get down and pray, but I have to say
that I disagree with the concept
of an "eye for an eye," when it means
that that old gook would get mine,
and all I would get back is his broken bean.

I Heard A Man Say

My genitals aren't worth blistering to
Chinatown smells like brown cheese

Old men still spit on sidewalk
while smoking cigarettes

next to bandaged sprinkler system
Obesity might not be the name

you sat down with
but it's never going to let you up

This could have happened anywhere
You don't need a disaster to know you are one

It's time to retire that smiling potato
No tomorrow to hang your hat on

When did happiness get so chewy
You have officially become an event

You look like you want
to end up in a trash bag

Sky full of half-bitten stars
Are we just a sack of crumbs

falling from one more catastrophe
I used to date a mannequin in a space suit

Whenever I look out the porthole
I can see the planet that ejected me

Is it because I am too human
or not quite human enough

Time to turn in old frequencies
Join other raincoats in a painting

No pain can reach me there

Something To Look Forward To

A blue and green city, with the sun rising behind it, just not swiftly enough
Don't worry about being perfect. Just make sure you have some juice left in the pump.

I have many other remedies on hand, not just history's bags of sumptuous soot
Hello, I am beauty's representative; I work in the self-improvement sector

Don't worry about being perfect. Just make sure you have some juice left in the pump.
How do you see yourself on the material plane of observed phenomena

Hello, I am beauty's representative; I work in the self-improvement sector
Have you ever been sideswiped by a bad investment in love

How do you see yourself on the material plane of observed phenomena
You might need a reevaluation, an estimate, or an era to expire

Have you ever been sideswiped by a bad investment in love
Before you decide that you are nothing more than a clump or splatter

You might need a reevaluation, an estimate, or an era to expire
Have you learned how to remove yourself from every mirror you pass

Before you decide that you are nothing more than a clump or splatter
Let me tell you about the palm trees on the horizon of your future

Have you learned how to remove yourself from every mirror you pass
A blue and green city, with the sun rising behind it, just not swiftly enough

Let me tell you about the palm trees on the horizon of your future
I have many other remedies on hand, not just history's bags of sumptuous soot

News Item

Recent polls suggest that escalating crescendos of frenzy still have to boil over before any resemblance to peace can be restored to the suburbs' last scamper towards *Paradise Hideaway* — the ultimate tier in vacation pleasure. Hiding in afternoon's tall shadows won't make it easier, while riding a stationary bicycle does not guarantee that you will obtain multiple lives or surplus personalities, as many have claimed. In fact, neither of these activities will help you commandeer a recreation vehicle of significant value so as to impress your bone-chewing neighbors. Daylight will continue to find its way to your door, open it, and enter in full regalia. And yes, you still have to go out at night for organic iceberg lettuce and vegan jelly donuts. For the time being, fisticuffs remain a popular form of entertainment among the young. Their parents and older siblings encourage it, having run this way before the latest wave of playthings arrived, their eyes shut tight, tired from the long journey begun in the jungles of tarmac darkness.

Dante's Carousel

Is this why you have taken me on a summer boating excursion
You cannot return to your old life in an empty bottle

Memory's blabbering children gather in a beer hall for one last nip
If I am going to get anything else done, I need to reassess my goals

You cannot return to your old life in an empty bottle
One day you are a poet with a future, the next day an unrepentant dog with a past

If I am going to get anything else done, I need to reassess my goals
When are tears more than a cloth soaked with soapy water

One day you are a poet with a future, the next day an unrepentant dog with a past
Whoever opens this box lets in the darkness that swells our tongues

When are tears more than a cloth soaked with soapy water
When did your poems start turning into stones

Whoever opens this box lets in the darkness that swells our tongues
If this crystal sends an answer, does that mean you no longer listen to the stars

When did your poems start turning into stones
This conversation is a perfumed goblet of sweetened rejection

If this crystal sends an answer, does that mean you no longer listen to the stars
Is this why you have taken me on a summer boating excursion

This conversation is a perfumed goblet of sweetened rejection
Memory's blabbering children gather in a beer hall for one last nip

Barnum and Bosch (1)

A new background is downloaded. Fuzzy vanilla curtain the townspeople can wrap themselves in, momentarily forgetting about the creatures waiting to pluck them from their narrow beds. Behind the half-eaten moon a fish waits to swallow whatever floats past. Alligators crawl out of a pond deep in the suburbs, led by an oily man in a straw hat.

I like sleeping under a flat stone, as it prepares me for the harness that lowers us deeper into the tunnel. We are hunting for telltale secretions, the after effects of denunciations.

Did I ever tell you about the time a monkey came up to me in a bar? It seems that he had been a donkey in his previous life and was wondering if there was any way for him to return to his barnyard antics.

Mail delivery has been temporarily suspended due to a lack of interest.

Or does all this happen after I wake up from a long sleep, convinced that everything has changed for the better. (Technically, this is called the rerun of a failed projection).

Or maybe this happens after I discover that my head has been turned in the wrong direction all along, like a doll owned by a girl with a malicious brother whose freckles got the better of him.

All plans are at standstill, a traffic jam with no solution. Virgil abandoned us long ago, preferring to offer guided tours of Hell and its ever-growing numbers of pedestrian walkways where suffering is a sitcom used to further distract the rich from those moments when nothing seems to turn out right for others.

Barnum and Bosch (2)

Fire rises from cavernous green mouth, long winding body trailing behind — slimy flag or dry fish. Nearby, a hand reaches toward a hand it cannot reach.

This brings up the question of whether or not you exist in someone else's dream if that person, unbeknownst to you, calls out your name in the dark, and the person or animal (if such is the case) lying beside said individual hears that string of sounds (vowels and consonants) in the order that they were intended? Or were they? Was that what was said or only what was heard? Maybe there was a distortion between the conception (dream) and the utterance (moan rising from mouth of sleeper to take shape in room).

Have you dialed in your request for divine assistance? Have you secretly nodded to someone whose red cloak covers all but his standard issue boots? Have you ever held a rock in your hand, hoping it would fly towards its intended target?

There is an institute where this hallowed domain of human behavior is closely examined, where courses are given, and daily lectures on a wide range of adjacent topics can be heard broadcast in the quadrangle: how to listen closely to your hormones when they get lonely; revelations of every color and persuasion and what to do with them; why you don't need to keep looking for an answer or even figure out what question you should be asking. Our goal is to have a lecture that can soothe every ailment, including those that have yet to glimmer on horizon's burnished rim. Are you ready to join the party? Or are you still reluctant to celebrate what can soon be yours?

Pan's Tomb

You never say the same things twice
This is a small problem you have with language

Everything has already been said, except by you
The moon is a chunk of gouda in the mouth of a rat

This is a small problem you have with language
The air is swarming with capillaries bursting with sound

The moon is a chunk of gouda in the mouth of a rat
I don't know my *head* from your *elbow* and it still hurts

The air is swarming with capillaries bursting with sound
A spoon made of silver hammered into a veined leaf

I don't know my *head* from your *elbow* and it still hurts
Why did you ask me to call your name if you don't know it

A spoon made of silver hammered into a veined leaf
A grasshopper tells a joke about yellow grass to a cricket

Why did you ask me to call your name if you don't know it
You never say the same things twice

A grasshopper tells a joke about yellow grass to a cricket
Everything has already been said, except by you

III.

After an Anonymous Student of Albrecht Durer and Hieronymus Bosch

Swirling groves inundated with ink impersonate a dream
in which delegations of extinct animals pursue you

By now neither natural and naked, nor artificial and armored
black lines brimming with branches of triumphant twitter

in which delegations of extinct animals pursue you
shot through with craving and lacking further content

Black lines brimming with branches of triumphant twitter
until green winds kiss the sea and scrolled waves turn red

shot through with craving and lacking further content
Your attempts to draw hounded by a violin of second thoughts

until green winds kiss the sea and scrolled waves turn red
You are not charged admission to witness these fantastic scenes

Your attempts to draw hounded by a violin of second thoughts
A pocket watch attached by wires to what looks like a bomb

You are not charged admission to witness these fantastic scenes
You are free to sink further into its residue of misery

A pocket watch attached by wires to what looks like a bomb
Swirling groves inundated with ink impersonate a dream

You are free to sink further into its residue of misery
by now neither natural and naked, nor artificial and armored

Written in the Shadow of Francis Bacon's *Self-Portrait Triptych* (1985-86)

1.
I haven't got a clue
as to why
I woke up
in these clothes
someone else's
cheaply manufactured
persona
bag of discounted
egg noodles
in one hand
throttling
dream's sweet neck
with other

2.
I still don't understand
how my face
ended up in the painting
that you are laughing at
while the rest of me
was tossed in the trash
Not even the bird
that whispers in my ear
knows the answer
to this ridiculous riddle

3.
And I still have no idea
why I am straddling
a broken tricycle
waiting for snow
to obliterate
this poem
Nor do I understand why
my declarations of love
are considered
unwarranted distractions
an annoying mosquito
full of venom
it doesn't know it is carrying

Written in the Shadows Cast by *The Burning of the Houses of Lords and Commons* (1835) by J. M. W. Turner

1.
At one point in the story the rain was green, and the sky was pink shot through with painterly streaks of mauve and gray. Everyone, including the servants and maids, went onto the verandah and began applauding. It wasn't yet evening.

Even those who were on the outside of the narrative — those like us, who had no place in the story — were invited to attend this momentous event.

Along the riverbanks the fulsome reflections of flowers blossomed in every imaginable hue. Some colors floated slowly toward the sky, like boats ferrying the dead to their destination. Twisted mazes of sparks led the way.

It was a celebration, an announcement of dread and joy. We were lost within a swirling storm of seraphic color, dripping with the revelations the sky had flung in our faces. That's when it came to our attention that the palace was on fire, but no one dared cross the river and approach its gates.

This was a different story, its narrative promising that the construction and destruction of civil order would occur naturally, like the weather or the flags flying within it.

This was the story none of us were invited to attend, unless we already had taken up residence in its chapters, with its stained pages rising toward the fiery ceiling the architect had told them would be blue forever.

This was the story that did not invite intervention.

2.

Just as there are two paintings, with many witnesses huddled on the far shore, there are at least two stories and those who weren't invited to listen to them.

This story happened before we met. No one but us remembers it now, two shadows standing beneath a stone arch, a dark river flowing past.

What does it mean to be alone with each other, sharing memories no one else has?

Or perhaps this is the story that cannot be addressed, the one that started with and without our consent, the one we are still telling, the one in which we become honorary citizens of a city not yet named.

Inhabitants of a small city, a hovel in the sky.

As it is, we are spoonfuls of ashes scattered among the day's abominations.

We will never be sure how our voices intersected amidst the pillars constantly being erected for and against prismatic densities by which one is supposed to swear lifelong allegiance.

Such alliances seemed based on a different astrology than the one guiding us through the night. There is another set of stars in the sky and we don't know their names or their purpose. That is what is pulling us across the burning lake.

This was a dream which one of us later told the other. Or dreamed of telling the other, as the difference between these two types of flying having dissolved long ago.

Each of us lay there thinking: I wish I could say something about our future that will come true.

3.

A room each of us wanted to erect, a story or shelter, against the wind that untethered us from everything we tried to hold onto, from concrete nodes to abstract ideas.

Each of us needed that shaded plateau, that place where sensual asides could unfold without interruption.

On the small shelves on which we pretended to sleep, when vast constellations of villainous orthography prowled the land, looking for components to evaporate into bursts of fiery laughter, we realized the world was porous, and that we were handfuls of sand trickling through its openings into the sea waiting below.

How to hold onto ourselves and each other without threatening the seedlings beneath the skin?

In the beginning we told ourselves there was an exit, somewhere for us to begin making up what had never happened and, in all likelihood, never would.

Later, we told each other in one way or another that there was a window with a view of paradise. We silently agreed that the window doesn't open because it was never there, but that the shadows of its imprint could be seen on the opposite wall. Some days we sit facing them, trying to decipher their promises, but more often than not, we look the other way, still believing that there is something else we need to see.

At the Tomb of Narcissus

Mirrors embrace so many lies you part company.
This minor moon, for example, praises a cratered face.

A greener visage hides inside a bird's panicked epithet.
I was raised to pay close attention to anonymity.

This minor moon, for example, praises a cratered face.
Do you see that I have two masks now? Neither is mine.

I was raised to pay close attention to anonymity.
Do you like this map of an orange shirt with four buttons?

Do you see that I have two masks now? Neither is mine.
This is my studio, my dream space. Do you belong here?

Do you like this map of an orange shirt with four buttons?
The earliest that you can become a stranger is now.

This is my studio, my dream space. Do you belong here?
I used to think that I could see the city from above.

The earliest that you can become a stranger is now.
It is necessary to sit in a room and tally the remaining comets.

I used to think that I could see the city from above.
I used to believe that roots spit flowers from their grave.

It is necessary to sit in a room and tally the remaining comets.
I am smiling, but I am not smiling — it is nearly twilight.

I used to think that roots spit flowers from their grave.
Mirrors embrace so many lies you part company.

I am smiling, but I am not smiling — it is nearly twilight.
A greener visage hides inside a bird's panicked epithet.

Firefly Promises

1.
Each of us began in mid-sentence, wiring frayed, blue electricity filling the air. Motion whispers anyone could see through if they stopped to look. This is the snapshot I see when I close my eyes. Faded music. Rush of disclosures followed by missives delivered in an electronic suitcase.

Walking on either side of the river of self-loathing, learning not to step into it, though we slip, and it is unavoidable. Later learning the names of those missteps so as not to make them again, though often did, as each said to the other in the future imperfect, from across the stream that widens and thins according to a tarot deck whose cards are never seen.

Reasons or excuses — which will we run out of first? Did we know when we started that the river was between us and that we drank from it, seeing not our reflection, but that of someone we didn't wish to resemble, even if we did. Some of this is real and some of this is oxygen. Details are crumbs and scabs to be picked at. A subsistence diet one could grow fat on.

What do you do with the fumes, the fuming, while scampering up the ladders of assuming? What disdain greets you, happy to welcome you home? What question that is already answered shall be asked of you next? Where is the rest of the bruised honey? Whose relic have you become? Why try on what doesn't spare you?

What was I just saying or thinking to say to you, the words hesitant, a smokestack unfolding its letters to the sky, which is always hurrying to the bus station full of wickedness and fast food? Am I capable of saying this? Or even this? Other than in mid-sentence, how I shall continue — knowing there is no end in sight.

This is not what the river told me would happen

2.
It is said that this is a human space we occupy, but today I am not so sure.

I wonder if we are in it or it is in us — a verb and a noun that have yet to announce their shapes or directions. Are we adrift or simply drifting?

Did we know that we would reveal ourselves so quickly? Did we know we would lead each other over valleys of pain because we didn't try to cover them, nor find any reason to call attention to their presence — they weren't monuments after all.

Sympathy wasn't what we wanted. That's what everyone asks for, a quick salve to bathe the deep ruins. It was as if all we wanted to do was start at the beginning and talk. Is such a beginning possible?

Had we guessed that other sentences would follow the first slow greeting, and the unexpected comfort of talking that began filling the air between you and I, between all the pronouns we occupied and abandoned?

Had we ever thought that it might be possible to talk about the pronouns we left behind, shed, buried, drove away, got rid of in a hurry? Or whisper about the ones we still carried with us?

Had we imagined the growing cascades filling missives sent from miles away, to someone sitting or driving, moving along a road the other would never see.

The only thing that holds us together are the missives we send each other.

Somedays the words seem even more real than we are.

It was as if I had never talked to anyone before. Or, it was that I had never talked to you before — talked to someone who seemed so open to what I was saying that the words appeared to fly through you. Your answers were not words, at least as I thought I knew them. They plunged into me, and they stayed wherever I looked. I began hearing them playing back.

I imagine this is what it must have been like for Odysseus when he had his crew tie him to the mast — music that not even music could describe. He must have kept hearing their notes long after the island vanished behind the horizon. Was that a crazy smile on his face?

3.

You have become a figment of my imagination telling me that whatever I wish for must remain unspoken. It is true that humans do not live on love alone. Bread and whiskey do not cover the rent. What do we become but scowling vacuum cleaners trying to clean the mess we have had made of our daily existence. The tell-tale crumbs of pointillist loathing are only part of the widening story that no one wants to tell.

The rest are gestures, celebrated poems, overactive prurience.

I decide it is better if I send a letter than a poem, a dream instead of a fiction, something dropped into the sea. This is by no means a testimony trudging ashore. Not even a poet's ego should be that grandiose.

Rather, it is a small corner of the page that I am trying to take up, a corner of a corner. On it I have written that one day I will watch you sleeping in my clothes. I don't know where this thought came from, but I have refused to put it away.

4.

I am copying down what I am being told to write. It is not a voice I hear, yours or mine or anyone else's, but the space between words that seems to fill with other words, other indications, hints or hums — a kind of music that words cannot accompany, falling away from their small handles on the world, like leaves on a windy day.

I am copying down what I am being told to write, but I keep thinking these are my words, not someone else's, that I am thinking and saying and sending to you. And yet it's not you that I am writing to, is it? It is my idea of you, my dream, illusion or glimpse. A string of silhouettes.

This can only mean that this is my ode to failing to write a poem worthy of your attention. Am I extolling you or extirpating words that are poor exposures of the quandary of pronouns you tell me constitute some of the parameters of your inexhaustible inferno?

Is this what it means to fall out of the unauthorized sky? Is this what it means to be a feather borne by the wind, or a cloud of thwarted eagerness? What brought us to this ocean of loneliness in which we can hear each other swimming in the distance?

Black Threads from Meng Chiao (1)

1.
Rickety lock
with arrow

drawn on its dimpled brass cover

scorpion
           dreaming

inside a paperweight

porcelain tub
white enamel stove

orange peel
           water bottle

beside a cutting board

tennis ball
           smiling

at its black reflection

painted bird
           flying beneath

cabinet keyhole
wooden chair
           wrinkled pants

torn drawing of a ship
manned by pirates

2.
Shall I float this poem on the river
to meet you

past the radiant light of oil refineries
the red neon glow of words rising above the horizon

past furniture outlets and cargo ships
lovers drifting towards the gorge

Shall I point this poem past weeds and overpasses
tents and chairs

past courtyards and parking garages
named after mythical animals

Shall I place this poem
on the swirling black river

in the last daylight hours
watching it turn

into clouds, mist and rain

3.
My room is filling
with butterflies and snow

An armless clock
cannot move slower

I don't need to part
the curtains

to know the sky behind it
is also black-and-white

a photograph of
a photograph

you sent me
via telepathic means

Whenever I close
my eyes

I hear rain's exploding
stars and tears

A photograph of you
burns its candle in my brain

I sit alone in my room
waiting for a poem

to appear in the shadows
I crawl into my tiny bed

a poet sleeping next to a cloud
I fill page after page with words

In the morning the paper is blank
This is how I send you my poems

written in dirt with a stick

Black Threads from Meng Chiao (2)

1.
In the bad translation of the Chinese poem
that I have all but forgotten

two lovers drift downstream in a boat
fashioned from ivory or teak

yellow tar or bald tires
an unlikely substance

which is true of love poems
written in a distant era

in purple mountains
populated by solitary archers

unemployed animal trainers
hermit poets searching for a lasting rhyme

I spend all day
talking to my shadow

It is winter or summer
I cannot remember which

Oil refineries send their candle flames jetting toward the moon
that old pearl

2.
I cannot
pen my shadow
to the page

Once the ink is dry
there will be no one
to read this poem

I might as well
count the leaves
falling from the sky

3.
Spring left when
I was not looking

Your beautiful translation
only makes my poem worse

Turning a few scattered lines
into fish darting beneath rocks

I heard you whispering to yourself
while the lovers drifted out of sight

Can you follow that red thread of sky
past junkyard piled with second-hand coffins

Petals from this poem
fall into black eddies

Weren't you once also a thick blue shadow
floating through the gorge

A column of snowy egrets
vanishes into the sun

If there was something
you could have held onto

what would it have been

Black Threads from Meng Chiao (3)

1.
Will this

                wandering

                              black thread

lead me

        to blue gorges

                          shrouded in mist

where I hear

        lovers drift in circles

                              beneath

thick clouds of smoky black ink

And moonlight

        fills rows of empty boats

2.
Will tracing

        this black thread

                dancing in my head

lead me to the lovers

           drifting in

                    their splintered sliver of a coffin

floating beneath

        balconies and pavilions

                    where poets boast to the moon

3.
Will grasping

        this black thread

                between my remaining teeth

lead me

        to the clouds of ink

              where

a voracious phoenix sleeps

The Detective's Love Letter

I was the detective in the book no one put down
that summer, in the red hills above Manhattan

You were different, even when you crinkled your nose
No brush could ever lift your face into view

that summer, in the red hills above Manhattan,
where trees lay scattered, like angels shot down from the sky

No brush could ever lift your face into view
The attraction you exerted upon me was uncanny

where trees lay scattered, like angels shot down from the sky
A light bulb shut off in mid-sentence

The attraction you exerted upon me was uncanny
We watched dolls gather to divide the spoils of war

A light bulb shut off in mid-sentence
Mr. Muddlehead counts his money in the dark

We watched dolls gather to divide the spoils of war
I dream that we stayed in a *pensione* in Pittsburgh

Mr. Muddlehead counts his money in the dark.
You grew rosier, while everyone else got nosier

I dream that we stayed in a *pensione* in Pittsburgh
It wasn't much, but it was something

You grew rosier, while everyone else got nosier
Nobody removed the excrement collecting around his or her thoughts

It wasn't much, but it was something
The sky offered a different testimony

Nobody removed the excrement collecting around his or her thoughts
I was the detective in the book no one put down

The sky offered a different testimony
You were different, even when you crinkled your nose

IV.
Egyptian Sonnets

Egyptian Sonnets

1.
Don't be vexed, dear jackals
Look upon this pavilion night,
where wounded statues murmur
unutterable things, and words
circle themselves like broken satellites
Strange devices harnessed with wings,
let your pages charm the charmed of our brief time,
hunkered down in their glow-worm hermitage,
sparkling with carrion: stars as thick as flies
— *subterranean cataract portal precipice bastion* —
fall through rifts of sky, and black foam
covers our dented prow's painted eyes
O my beloved, look through your tears and your cries,
heaven still sits inside a gem copied
                                        in pomegranate and vermillion

2.
A hippo sits patiently in a palm tree
while a hoopoe hops up a ladder
On desert's edge, far from flickering
oil lamps, a Sloughi plays tag with jackals
a leopard herds gazelles and geese
with a jeweled flute, and a young lady rat,
sitting on a pearl throne, waits
for monkeys to slide forth their gifts
A lion and a fox visit a sick ibis
A hyena stops a goose from running
into its mouth, and panthers stand petrified
in front of a white cat ambling toward the library
The first idol was a goddess
with a body of a hippopotamus

3.
Before cursing that there is no canopic jar to piss in:
You, sleeper who is awake, why not listen
For above you are clouds of solitary voices
streaming toward glassy surface
of a page gleaming in sand
And right there, before you
write there: *Trampling, splashed*
a masquerade by the one
whose lips are on fire
Tumultuous throng fidgets
in folds above green shore
What mirage brought you to me
clothed in a sigh of loathsomeness
riding a crocodile, golden head held high

4.

Listen, turquoise crocodile dreaming of swine,
and you too, my trembling agate hyena,
this agile beetle leaves no trail in the mud,
and these butterflies turn to blue ash
falling from the roof of this bloodstained sky
Listen, Baby Buzzard and Uncle Osprey,
this beetle has neither eyes nor a mouth
when a young boy jags open his dog
with a dagger's bright lightning
Listen, *Wheredidyougo* and *Whatdoyoumean*
I will never sing your secret names again
Listen, o my dearest charioteer,
I am flying towards your eviscerated heart
Onyx smoke rises from my ruby eyes

5.

Horizon helmet horse hierophant
Sun presses clay snakes back
into rows of snarling eyes
Bristles brings back their prey
Red tent clouds lifting wings
Blue wizardry of lizards falling from
mouth of lion mounted in umber sky
By the time you reached me, I was fading
Into paint; dust lips were all that remained
Moon's prim carcass, black star's
framed mirror pulled by chariot
Dog circle imprint shadow
I cannot stop and look back
I should have carved my name
                              into your open face

6.

Do you copy each hour of the double horizon,
its gold torso, azure head, and emerald light
Another bandaged sun bleeds into rivers,
proud to have bequeathed its demonic power
to dust and air. Are you oar and heir
Do you recline among lizards and lions
Black-and-yellow heaven accompanies this worm-eaten boat
through plumes of sulfurous battle smoke
Sky's one-armed charioteer sings: *O brief insect,*
dying in wingless and windless day, do our hearts dilate
before outlines dissolving in tears and sand
I grow among flowers; Dweller in Dust is my name
I rise from a couch of snow atop a rotting mountain
I make my nest in the rafters of a falling sky
but you (and only you) stand naked and alone
                                        in a public fountain

7.

Dog-headed moon clutches palette
packed with styli, an invitation
to cross into kingdom of glyphs,
those sandals that follow our shadows
into dreams, pits and caverns,
cavorting and thwarting, plazas
and boulevards, avenues quiet,
except for unspeakable night
bleeding in the mouth of its beloved,
fiery madness darting from scarlet eyes,
summer's sweet smell of tar,
dust of daffodil stars
sinking to bottom of sky's smoky river

8.

Moon's misshapen hand
Moth after moth's gathered dust descends,
wrenching you from lure of secret spells
And along deserted aqueducts,
where frog and deer tongs
remove vials of human crust,
you learn to gird yourself
beside rising sands
No other time and place
to sing this song
O Broken Lullaby
I carry the shadow I cannot marry
as sun's wagon
topples its contents into charcoal sea

9.

Clear-eyed fish trickle of blood and mist
Cormorant moon in slow decline
Clouds dyed brown in night's overgrown arbor,
some wind-wandering fragment of ink
dropped into sky's broken jar, my homage to you
Sun's anvil embers, constellations's emerald hair
I carve silhouettes into sand
Now I stand so very still, alone on a little hill
Time, that patient curse, combs the furze
and scrawls letters on horn-headed breeze
Amidst midnight hubbub bubbling above
a mountain flakes into stone tears
Lucid torments return to their original bodies
attired entirely in broken reflections

10.
Night, dispassionate scholar of our fears
opens its portfolio, and unwraps
our bracelets of tears again
How ghostly this train,
quiet as a forest,
hung about in smoke
And a poet,
in a sudden fit,
falls weeping
A monstrous serenity,
rainbow salts, smooth lipped,
the sculpture frozen in oratory,
lunar horns spreading
from its silver forehead

11.

A human jar
with coiled hair
bathes his osprey stump
in fountains of wind-divided rain,
chatters, stamps, and trumpets
as if triumphant, like gold mist
brushed over pearl-encrusted mountains
Each visit to the clouds suspends leaves and buds
Night's sapphire bow is locked up again
And on the facing wall
the poem releases
its syllables
inside a burning house,
its walls of red and rising water

12.

I burn your wasp-coiled hair,
extricate your eyes from their nests,
axe the prows pointing toward black tomorrow
Disrobed, wings shorn off,
I join the dead
                         My body stands in line
with those who ask to have their memories
murdered and buried beside them,
in jars that barely raise their rims above the sand
Small and invisible, even to myself,
I stop calling out
the names of my loved ones
Plants become hieroglyphs
lined up on a branch
                                It is cold
Rabbits run across the sky

13.

Constellations' circulatory system,
possessed by magnetism of repulsive
and attractive forces, some
indistinguishable from
their snout-nosed brethren,
who, under moon's blue fresco,
ascend with their scroll of amorous requests,
while smoke nests in eaves of crooked sky
Impossible to dream all night
without quivering in treacherous air,
this spasm of time
through which we pass,
each pressed by love's calamities
as regions of sky arrive and depart

14.

Maroon stars dipped in caves where ochre lizards sleep
O Roofless Night, what vantage point
can be gained from these poems
that does not appease you
                                      I am afraid

This wooden pillow swallows all tears
How silly to think that words
can escape through the loopholes
of their dungeons
Is it better to leave
our story untold,
to be eagle, snake, or goat
circling its own cold tomb,
when these songs inherit incoming sky,
its paper, pen and ink -- its cold clay clouds

15.
Stars deposit insect-ravaged canopy
Moon unfastens its crimson mask
Dust-jacketed voices crackle storm clouds
gathering within
                          Blue laughter
mounts the podium; in a deserted airport
alone with my coffee and spiral donut,
a dead lamb lumped at my feet
Whose childhood shadow
am I here to escort to the slaughterhouse
Whose smoke-filled chambers
shall I enter, head bowed to tessellated snakes,
an unassigned scribe who adores you,
with broken hands
beneath gouged-out eyes

16.

Why stop and shudder
in stone lull by river,
when we can float over granaries
full of taxations, dawdle in
Alley of Hangman's Rope,
read Papyrus of Farewells
Why refuse vulture's perfume
osprey's red powder,
when we can scrawl
our epithets in water
Why dwell on twinkling
crystalline madness
Why please you
when names can remove the stars
                        from the poem

17.
Awakened by pigeons
made rich by undigested jewelry
Cloak of brown goat yarn,
clad only in sandals and necklaces.
burdened with salt
Babanus, ebony, mahogany, and acacia
On frescoes, turns as it turns now,
lions, giraffes, and hippos
Pastel blue, grey-green, orange with blue-
green, pink and violet beneath the clouds,
In cigarette smoke and yellow vapors
bronze-brown, tall, gaunt, all muscle
and sinew, cavernous and cadaverous
far from the granite enemy, almost vertical

18.

As if awakened by a signal we cannot hear,
quivering tufts, flashing metallic plumage,
ibises practice stretching their necks.
Brown geese become old-fashioned governesses
and storks gather, like unemployed advisers
while pelicans turn into roughly piled
walls of yellow-pink stones,
stout professors, now philosophical
now screaming in argument
collecting fish after fish, just as children
cram berries in their pockets
Silver arrows darting into undergrowth
Some run on foot the whole way
The sea compels them to rise into air

19.
An airplane hovering above a postage stamp
Enslaved, sold, oppressed, in revolt,
tricked and then trampled
The plow has not yet gained its iron nose
In churned expanse, where camels sink
up to their knees, hard quartz hills
Charcoal stacked in layers
Dry ropes break, lemons packed in tin
In a botanical garden dotted with
blossoms of blood, secluded women
watch travelers carrying gifts into the desert,
watch strangers tear white feathers
from ostriches, watch haloes shrink
and darkness thicker than blood roll in

20.
Rhododendrons' metallic rosettes
Bouganvilleas' dull purple
Light refracted from jasmine and oleander,
all colors sink into an emerald luster
The prophet's color is green
All the wanderer's longing
descends into it; dreams of coolness,
secluded quiet of home and bed
Turtledoves coo from mango trees
Hoopoes of Hafiz hop in fan palms
and Horus, caught in golden turquoise-blue,
utters his all too brief declaration of love
Far below him earth's broken garden goes on
while above him the upholstered sky rolls by,
                                            an irritated dream

21.
The archer aiming the arrow
is a peacock
pierced by love,
writes the scribe
on hem of night sky
Smoke Mausoleum Winter
Marsh Huckabuck Reef
Nest Instruments Messenger
And in the story unfolding below,
on the facing wall:
Caught inside its cage,
who knows
this other race we become,
as we peck furiously at bread sky

22.

A headless figure
once stood
proud and spindly on this plaster pedestal,
engraved with the title: *Painter*
Repeatedly cursed in daily ceremonies
Believed to have once had
a dripping snout,
long corkscrew ears
Reported to possess
curious compound-eyes
Known to reject all
manifestations of description and deception
except in cases where they are deemed necessary
such as *the impossible now*

V.
Bijoux in the Dark

Biopic

In those years of lost sunlight and hidden shadows — when pain was mirrored in the sepia puddles that gathered after outbursts from the sky — stylishly dressed pilgrims strode past mounds of dirty dishtowels bunched up by the side of the road leading to the capitol.

No one remembers seeing taxis or rickshaws cruising the streets spreading beyond the golden-domed towers clustered in a circle, like eggs in a nest. Something stood still, but it wasn't time. Planes remained stationary in their hangars. Trains slowly converted to rust in the railway yards. If you got your hands on a chicken — which few ever did — you could use the glove compartment of an old car to cook it.

This was during the era when children sold their aged parents on every corner, and those that didn't found another way of tricking them into leaving their apartments, and wandering unsupervised through the cobblestone streets in search of a fitting distraction. All the curtainless windows were empty.

This is the setting in which the following story unfolds. According to one of the many biographies — all unofficial and unsubstantiated, of course — the actor stopped answering the phone at the height of his fame, not when his aura began to fade.

One morning, he fired his agent and moved to another city — beyond the horizon approached by pilgrims — where he rented the maid's quarters from an elderly woman who never went to the movies. Located at the top of a column of spiraling stairs, it was a perfect way for him to begin a new life. There was a rocking chair and spider plant on the iron balcony. He read books he borrowed from the library and seldom looked up. He learned that the Sunday choir music from the church across the street came in shards, choreographed by a famous organ master.

Nauseated by the music's intricately choreographed attempt to uplift everyone's heart, the ex-actor reluctantly left his nest behind and moved to an abandoned missile silo on the outskirts of a region known for its wine and vinegar. He descended into his concrete hole and only occasionally emerged.

Dotted with lavender and lilacs, this landscape is where they met, of course. Which makes sense, since the surrounding geography afforded them a beauty they could not have witnessed elsewhere.

A teacher of Latin and Greek, she was the youngest daughter of an anarchist — a braided breeze in a prehistoric cave.

Some townspeople claim that — shortly after they were married — she began painting her husband's portrait every few days. The finished ones were stored in her father's barn, all facing toward the wall. Marie, her oldest niece, once told the postmaster that her aunt intended to burn down the barn the morning after her husband died, it didn't matter what season. She planned on mixing both his ashes and the barn's with water, churning up a grainy sludge she could use to make drawings.

A roving minstrel passed through town and told the couple what they could count on, but he was wrong.

They held hands, and then they held each other. This escalation of intimacy follows the rules handed down to us by our ancestors, but for them something unexpected happened and no one knows what it is.

These are a few of the clues we have. They opened a gas station and sold barbecued pork ribs on Sundays. For years, on bright Sundays, they jumped off a cliff into the ocean and walked back to town. They are said to have learned how to change horses in midstream but never did this to show off. They never got tattoos, as was the custom of the people living in this region. They swept up their friend's ashes and placed them in the proper container.

Years later, as they were dwindling into their separate heaps — dishtowels to be left by the side of the road — a casually dressed, perfectly groomed, middle-aged man with an embossed card, an exceedingly handsome chauffeur, and a shiny limousine drove into town. He offered to buy the movie rights, but they politely refused, much to the consternation of those gathered at the next table.

All this happened during the summer of the anaconda and tapir, evenings of heat lightning followed by winding passages of orchestral rain.

Movie Night

We were eating the latest wave of migrant sausages mixed with rare spices on the black verandah of the *Flying Saucer Bar and Grill* when I heard someone telling you that there was a rumor that I had sex with you once, but, at that point in your life, you weren't paying attention to small interruptions, and that, despite the peaks and valleys one naturally must traverse, nothing untoward happened, though an event unfolded (call it the collision of time and space dotted with foreign objects), what it was no one can now recall, even though someone said that he had heard that I had set out on a journey from the far end of town to tell you that what had happened that day was better than anything that could be said about it, but this is a different person that is speaking, the one who wasn't in the backseat intersecting with you, upright in the dark, but was sitting hunched over in the front cavity, driving through villages and towns scattered beneath the stars, haphazard collections of artificial light squatting in the dark, swarmed over by nothing they can remember, as the vehicle careened past libraries, firehouses, and general stores, repositories locked up for the night, two people curled around each other, pushing themselves into that place where shedding is inevitable, no one gripping the steering wheel, as the malfunctioning starship wobbles deeper into the dark, but of course this isn't what happened the night it happened there were two bodies and many shadows (some of them benign) embracing them in the parking lot beneath a yellow streetlamp near a train station occupied by two puppets on stilts, in the distance a blue castle commanding all who could see it to obey, kneel before its authority, yes there are instances, even now, when a tessellated edifice appears on the horizon or a child with one leg and an old sword hobbles out into the street, not to be run over by the tram, all while the two of them or is it us are engaged in a criminal act, at least as such acts are defined by the owner of the castle, a bald figurine whose corkscrew mouth never stops twisting, even in sleep, can't you hear what is happening outside, lightning on the rim of the world, arrival of thunder, the bowling alley shaking under the weeping willow, and there we are in the middle of a sentence that joins us and won't let go, and the longer we stay in this sentence, this rain, the more gets poured out of the containers that constitute our separate physical manifestations, including those things that we have never said to ourselves before, which is how all this got started.

Shipboard Entertainment

I suspect that many of us — who are taking this getaway cruise for the first time — have already heard that there is a blue cloud swirling through every media outlet, headlined by the report that last Sunday a fleet of UFOs was seen flying across our capital's searchlight skies, but neither puffy pink pundits nor tanned television anchors and their slim, velvety smooth sidekicks have been able to satisfactorily explain how — in the middle of this latest polarizing commotion, its unsavory imbalance of flames and fluids — wayward individuals, such as ourselves, have gained a wide array of new and unlikely talents while sailing in carefully plotted circles: today, with carefully aimed kicks, we are able to separate pointed flames from the fat cylindrical candles that the crew has graciously set up around the perimeter of the beautifully appointed stateroom: we can sing popular songs that we have never sung before, and, in some cases, are only now hearing for the first time as the words emerge from our mouths in perfectly tuned order, but if this is — as some among us suspect — an introduction to the collective nightmare that is waiting for us in the days ahead, I think many of us might look forward to it: not all of us, of course — that young couple dancing in the back, for instance, the ones that looked like they just stepped out of a best-selling detective novel, those inky surrogates for our neon desires and midnight fantasies, a string of indulgences that we often try to avoid further stimulating, as they will only lead us deeper into the glittering pleasure dome, that spiral of descent into pandemonium's maze, where we dream of attaining a state of gratification, however temporary, that many citizen claim to forego, choosing instead to embrace life's daily pressures and letdowns, at least that is what the bright brochure that brought us together announces, but isn't there a loophole in this narrative and all the others being broadcast, a widening crack that desperadoes — meaning us — use to enter another story closer to the one of their own making, even if it takes place in a deserted underground garage, or in a mirrored elevator that makes unscheduled stops on unnumbered floors, or on the sagging porch of a yellow beach bungalow surrounded by unimaginable hostilities, surely you and I — whoever we might be in this imagined life — would have met by now, no matter which puppeteer is directing the action: otherwise we would be greeting guests at a golf course, or tending flowers in a former cemetery, or guarding a wrought iron entrance against the complications that come with sickness and old age, but no, that is not us, because we have chosen to be the ones in the corner of the painting — near where the artist planned to put his signature but didn't, no one knows why — reborn as the gambling younger sister of a crime boss and an apprentice in office lighting systems, or a cryptic ruffian and a smart aleck agent, or a blackballed poet and a debauched vicar — the combinations are as numberless as the stars — or shall we continue on as before, avoiding all mention of the unprincipled wolf packs prowling the deck of our icebound ship, while we wait patiently for the magician's latest act to glue us to our seats.

Ten Successful Adventure Movie Formulas

1. Samurai enters town looking for gas station because he wants to water his horse.

2. Sunset: bubblegum, rose, and cinnabar shootout on circular roof of iconic high-rise — surrounded by lush blooms of orchid and teal plantings — culminates in blood-soaked trilby and partial amnesia.

3. After finding a misshapen doll in cigar box, a pimply adolescent discovers that he is endowed with an array of superpowers, accompanied by intoxicated feelings of superiority periodically riddled with outbursts of uncontrollable whimpering.

4. She realizes that it is easier and more efficient to drain this drunken leech of his tendril resources rather than trying to unscrew the cap of his bottled-up emotions.

5. He is hired to berate his shadowy undercover partners for their idiocy, which soon leads them to wandering through a warren of abandoned concrete bunkers looking for a lost girl and her favorite cat.

6. After her mentor dies of a mysterious illness, she must find someone equally unscrupulous to help her maintain control of the big production bosses.

7. The tattoo, which can only be glimpsed through binoculars, tells the story of a young man destined to marry a gambler with a mysterious history dating back to an automobile manufacturer suspected of espionage and murder.

8. Burly and chivalrous mobster with a titanium spear gun, corrupt nightclub chanteuse, cigar-chomping wolf with elegant hind legs, and worthless immature troublemaker — these are some of the unforeseen ways to debunk any manifestation of manic ruckus before the climax gets out of hand and real blood is spilled down the alley way.

9. Surplus captivity should be displayed in the first inundation, but after that it becomes merely commendable, no matter how realistic the sonic ambience.

10. Poisoned or poisonous — start with the one that speaks to you most and go on from there.

Ten Famous Outtakes

1. Before a retired, lovesick assassin embarks upon making a detailed list of his Machiavellian shenanigans, dating back to early childhood, he decides it might be best to study cryptography

2. Velvet ropes are used to suspend a beautiful but unscrupulous inventor above a vat of rotting perfume where rats frolic in the steam

3. A sultry, air-stirring singer asks her one-eyed boss to empty the ashtray before exiting her dressing room

4. An elderly astronomer opens the bedroom window of his remote summer cottage and discovers a dead falcon lying on the sill, holding an indecipherable message in its beak

5. After shaving her head, the award winning actress decides to settle for a small, wordless role so that she can make an offer that no one — not even the film's director — will be able to refuse

6. A girl biker gang whose members wear red leather cowboy hats is last seen driving across a bridge that didn't exist yesterday

7. The students ignore the warnings issued by a group of stern faculty until they discover one of their classmate's heads buried in the schoolyard

8. After the traitor forgets to send the truck careening over the cliff, he drives home where his wife and two adoring daughters run to greet him

9. A failed bigwig thinks it might be time to become a writer after stealing a manuscript from a dying street peddler

10. A deranged swordsman returns to the village where he was born, to look for his twin brother who — everyone tells him — never existed

Ten Enduring Statements from Lost or Forgotten Films

1. It was like our souls got sucked through a straw and what was waiting on the other side was a preliminary sketch of the future.

2. It is not every day that you can pick out your poison and be happy with the results.

3. Listen, will you — it doesn't matter if you've never seen anything like this before: No one is going to believe you anyway.

4. I've seen your face someplace before, and I don't like where I seen it.

5. Just look around — we got photos of every catastrophe imaginable and that's not all.

6. The law requires them to keep you alive until they are sure you are dead.

7. Death isn't a brick wall but a racing bike with a bent back rim.

8. I start getting concerned when I feel the cool mud rise between my ears.

9. What happens when you learn that your first language has been put on a ventilator?

10. You are destined to make the headlines; you just don't want to read them.

Bijoux in the Dark

The film was rumored to have disintegrated, but that was not the case. A copy of it existed in the library of the small town where the director had been born and where he was last seen entering a theater that has become a minor but enduring monument to his artistry.

According to the descendants of those who first saw the film, some of them many times, the story was not the main reason why they returned over and over again to the theater, to sit in the dark and watch the characters make their way across a silver tundra that was clearly fake, survive innumerable catastrophes that were staged, and, in some cases, under rather preposterous conditions demanded by the machinations of an improbable plot, and — fulfilling what one critic referred to as the classic dénouement — fall in love without their every movement toward each other having been accompanied by music, it was that none of this happened as it had been carefully planned, blocked in, and rehearsed; that accidents of all kinds kept sneaking in, like a three-legged dog that manages to run off with the Sunday ham and not lose the slice of pineapple and maraschino cherry that have been attached to it by the slimmest of means.

Legend has it that the dog made it to a traffic island on the other side of town where it was able to devour the pineapple slice without disturbing either the cherry or the ham, which is a Class A type of unexpected occurrence shooting through the film's darkest crevices, its painted lightning bolts jagging deep into the mineshaft down which we all occasionally tumble, like Alice, once we emerge from the theater and step out onto the busy street — automobiles from another century buzzing by.

The more intrepid members of the audience reported that they made their way to the Empire Diner for a dinner consisting of a small green salad, chicken croquettes, mashed potatoes, and string beans that are never green. Chocolate pudding provided the right conclusion for some, while others preferred the bread pudding topped with a dollop of creme fraiche. It seems that no one asked for coffee, because they did not want to miss out on their dreams, those little pockets of irresponsibility.

You and I took a different route, and, like the heroes of the film, we ended up facing the prospect of crossing a mesa filled with snow. In the distance was a small farmhouse, smoke curling lazily up from its sturdy chimney.

The camera zoomed in, and the close-up followed.

A man came out on the porch, followed by two small children and a cat. Each of them waved, but the children seemed sad, and the circular motions their hands made was clearly an action that they had repeated many times before. They were methodically trying to wipe clear a window to see what was approaching from the other side. For those in the audience, this moment, where we began hovering in the air, as if we were butterflies or birds floating above the story that was running beneath us, is what we still talk about when the oven is warming up, and our hands sift through the flour as if it is hiding something that that has been misplaced or lost.

Film Reviewer

The film reviewer attained cult status, his writing prized by many readers. His fans looked forward to Wednesday evenings, to savoring his precise but not precious prose and the nuggets contained therein. His recommendations helped them plan out their weekend. And then he did the inexplicable: he began writing about movies that were never made. Or he was writing about films that were lost, or existed only as rumors, or never amounted to more than failed schemes. He reviewed them as if they were real, which, of course, they were.

Many of his fans were puzzled by his refusal to distinguish between what he had seen and what he could not have seen, even as they continued to bask in the mellifluous arrangement of vowels and consonants he offered up to them, week after week. No one else came as close as he did, to describing the sensuous pleasure of sitting alone in a darkened theater — anonymous as an unidentified shadow in a murder mystery. No one else rendered — with such sculptural fire and sonic flights — the intense delight of watching the interplay of light and shadow, and what happened when every surface was doused with color.

Not all the movies the film reviewer saw got positive notices. In those theaters the seats remained empty, the light shining back on an empty room. Occasionally he urged his readers to seek out a film, which might be playing briefly in an out-of-the-way cinema. Some made the trek, while others — the majority — let it vanish into the borrowed air, seldom seen again. For some fans — especially the ones who had gotten on in years — his writing began to replace the movies he was writing about. They didn't need to deal with public transportation, or with possible mishaps. They could stay at home, or wherever it was that they had taken up residence, and read the review: the worthy surrogate.

There is the fanged mouth that feeds on loose ends. We wonder if this is what heaven is like — an old movie theater with thick velvet curtains that part, as the lights dim and the naked cherubs peering down from the blue and gold ceiling vanish, like comets. Surely, this must be the place the film reviewer is asking us to find: the room where lost movies are restored to their former glory, and where we are invited to make detours that not even our dreams take us on.

VI.

Other Local Delights

This morning, Mister Skunk, taxi driver extraordinaire, found his piggy bank broken
Simpering accusers, it is not yet your turn, and the sky is still bitter gray

You need to open your eyes and grasp what you have let in
It is useful for children to experience firsthand how Goblins cook blizzard eggs

Simpering accusers, it is not yet your turn, and the sky is still bitter gray
Even if this is the moonshine factory where spotted beetles mate

It is useful for children to experience firsthand how Goblins cook blizzard eggs
Never follow your heart, but always wear a civilized mask and smile

Even if this is the moonshine factory where spotted beetles mate
A bucket of tepid pee and a pyramid of biscuits will do you good

Never follow your heart, but always wear a civilized mask and smile
A favorable impression does not translate into damaged collateral

A bucket of tepid pee and a pyramid of biscuits will do you good
This poem was written while sitting under a zeppelin of despair

A favorable impression does not translate into damaged collateral
Before you turn into a worm, might I slip this business card into your mouth

This poem was written while sitting under a zeppelin of despair
This morning, Mister Skunk, taxi driver extraordinaire, found his piggy bank broken

Before you turn into a worm, might I slip this business card into your mouth
You need to open your eyes and grasp what you have let in

Different Drum

> "In Dreams Begin Responsibilities."
> —*Delmore Schwartz*

In dreams begin irresponsibilities
Elliptical plummets on wind's back
Reels and rolls
Lost footage
Folded and torn snapshots
Exits bolted
Heat molded telephone
Rotting inside story
What will it be
Old flames
Burning postcards
Crooked black cradles
Donut's toxic modules
Sweet parade dust
Sputtering in cooperation room
Down from where
You are a scientist
Or a druggist
Billiard idiot
Or pool shark
A head wound
With blue ascot
In cordovan and corduroy
Crunch of caravan
Pressing nose
Against earth
Cupid's broken left arm
Slings more arrows
Than you can spit on
Grant this poet
This wheezing pariah

This purveyor of riddled language
This impecunious slug
This soiled stew pit
This chop suey commercial
Tattooed status of blue stethoscope sky
Poisonous petals growing in vats
Dotted ursine lump
Borrowed archer
Blessed be these
Bits of glassy grime
Morning coolness
Twirling butterflies
Biographical vapors
Skywriting under the trees
Special attention
Must be paid
To journeying
Along narrow paths
Between Santa and Satan
Samarkand and Sausalito
Between monastically cropped lawns
Raising their spikes in triumph
Snapped open and released
Almanacs cataloguing
Temptations salvations redemptions
Averted and advertised
Icy blue sonnets
Corseted couplets
Meticulously cut cubes of cheese
Poetry of obligatory peephole
Poetry of commonplace
Sorrow made special
Attention calling
Intricacies of divorce
Desertion disaster
Island of scholarly flocks
Pork barrel and beans

The carcass is a remnant
What fled the scene
Dragging its tongue
Across earth to no avail
Windows nailed
Shut in yellow clay
Doors burned
To their shadows
Copious ashes
Boomeranging
Across barn
Slain brethren
Amending backyard
Barbecue pits
Determined inhabitants
Hatched in spectrum
Calculated range of
Normalized behavior
Substitute underworld arcade
Incarcerated conversation
Daughter of a cancer
Son of an egregious terror
There are many ways
To repeat yourself
This is not one of them
This is fragrance skipping amok
Amidst sacred hydrocarbons
Scintillation of metallic water
Graffiti: Poets are germ engravers
Disguised as grave diggers
Graffiti: Dawn is a seagull
Stuck on far end of plastic fork
Graffiti: Plenum of glabrous vampires
Await further distribution
Gleaming pink arrangement and camera shy
Using only long ropes and sharpened pegs
Ban the use of euphemisms

This poem will not extol
Virtues of one-room schoolhouse
Bootstrap dragging
Pulley mechanism
Grand pasha of motivating metaphors
Heated by potbellied
Police officer
Spoonfuls of coal dangled
Into mouth of glowing ghosts
Flocking at door of meaning
Trumpet clock's composition of anxiety
Notoriously unwilling to offer
Proper burial services
Plagiarism plagued provinces
Egyptian garage complete
With gas-operated chariot
Whalebone bathtub
And muslin shawl
Do not slobber on yourself
In an attempt to be
Distracting and beautiful
Do not paraphrase
Your green fatty regions
They are lectures
On inevitability of collapse
Do not pretend
To fabricate frivolity
Just another post in worm fence
Do not dance around bride
Toiling at her daily bread
Claiming I was not myself that day
— Or anyone else for that matter —
Time travel is a popular
Vacation resort
Vacated escort
Where thinking
Becomes a form of relief

A polka dot rain cloud
Attempting to communicate
With pink mesa
Ladled blue
Pheremones
Pilgrims dutifully trudge across
Six-lane highway of higher education
Enter great rotunda
Each sucking a lozenge
Blessed impediment
Granted imperceptible privileges
Summer accentuates colors
Found in parking lots
Drive-through commuter carpet
Majestic mauve
Not among them
The air you breathe
Becomes iron
Free collar
Grammatical reaction
To inherited condition
Corruption engines
Steaming stacks of paper
Waiting to greet you
Beat you at end of long journey
Poem trafficking in words
Circling mountains of shoes and shirts
Dentures from another time and place
Charnel house archive
Weather conjuring
Spiral dregs
Character development
No longer
Part of the syllabus
Consigned to
Bevy of blonde-colored bleachers
Flooded with glissando pigments

This is not the right
Time to imitate nausea
Unhitch your wagon
From horses of irritability
Gallant knights
Melt in merciless sun
Daylight's rubber eraser
Sticking more
Pink dust to your lips

Overnight

In Memory of Paul Violi (1944 – 2011)

I did not realize that you were fading from sight
I don't believe I could have helped with the transition

You most likely would have made a joke of it
Did you hear about the two donkeys stuck in an airshaft

I don't believe I could have helped with the transition
The doorway leading to the valleys of dust is always open

Did you hear about the two donkeys stuck in an airshaft
You might call this the first of many red herrings

The doorway leading to the valleys of dust is always open
The window overlooking the sea is part of the dream

You might call this the first of many red herrings
The shield you were given as a child did not protect you

The window overlooking the sea is part of the dream
One by one the words leave you, even this one

The shield you were given as a child did not protect you
The sword is made of air before you knew it

One by one the words leave you, even this one
I did not realize that you were fading from sight

The sword is made of air before you knew it
You most likely would have made a joke of it

Standard Operating Procedure

Dissatisfactions are on the rise, starting with the texture of bread, the color of coffee, the decay of cheese, none of which fit the bill, while all is made more interminably repellant by the seats one encounters in pubic accommodations. You must be prepared for the worst, even while accepting that things will sink much further; that there is no bottom to the bottom.

There are myriad examples of this that I need not visit, at least here, as their present whereabouts are well known. Say what you want, even if you aren't convinced that you mean it. Here is the intersection.

I have left my fishing boat to founder on the rocks, thrown my keys into a littered field, and stopped eating in restaurants that advertise their riches.

You can decipher these actions by any code that you think fits. I am not one to decide how things should be read. But let me assure that there is far more to be done, even if I am not the one to do them. This is what is meant by the unavoidable reduction to essentials.

Three, Not Four Seasons

This swimming pool,

that fur coat

and,

further back,

in the reddening twilight,

another valuable carcass

draped about bared shoulders,

soft as the caress

citizens imagine is theirs to administer

in a time of moaning need.

These iniquities are commonplace.

The rest is not gravy.

Pockets of perfumed air squander obscenities

whenever they squawk into their cellular devices,

thinking there is an ear of magnitude on the other side.

Pandemonium waits to spring from the sky.

Sanctuary sits in the dark

a burning dollhouse crammed with seraphs.

Cash is its own award.

Advice to the Love Worn

Welcome to tonight's special installment
The one and lonely
Babylonian Baloney
Soap Opera
Coming to you
Live and on fire

O Sumerian high spot
Your recent spout
Got me head-locked
In crackup mode

But this storm of machine display huffing
Is a prize
No one would drink of administering
To a vacated mannequin
Much less shovel inside totem
Tattooed with outline of extinct blue aphrodisiac

Maybe you should rethink your objectives
Based on remaining tent stakes
Holding down last reality flaps

Perhaps you should pen a confessional poem
In which one of you is afflicted (or conflicted?)
With gobs of properly vetted sorrow
While the other (the Other!) hugs
Latest example of imported dignity

Call it the human equation factor
And add *Lachrymose*
(Not, lack remorse)
To your vocabulary of hot spots

You too have learned to bake
Unfortunate omissions
Into an admirable lie
Build towering wet rind
Plastered with gold stars and wolf whistles

In the meantime, however, you should
Practice your composure
Adjust your public valve release,
Check on inner corpse
Bobbing convulsively
In far and foreign corners

Remember
Exercises in patience
Are a controlled form
Of delayed gratification
For the greater good

Angry Birds

Yes, I am a cartoon
a cartoon of small birds flying from my mouth
their wings beating ferociously against the wind
small birds too slight to carry syllables seething inside my brain
strangled sounds I cannot enunciate with syllabic clarity
their garbled wings beating and beating
against cold air of disapproval

This behavior is not appropriate
You must change direction immediately
Turn away from these small birds
this beating and beating
on an otherwise peaceful day whose peace is all in the mind

Small birds fly from my mouth en route to you
Poems enmeshed in sounds I cannot enunciate
These sounds flying from my mouth
covered in spit
my life's blood

Coda

Midway

I did not write a hauntingly beautiful book
No one was haunted by the words I wrote
Neither they nor the book were beautiful

I did not write a book in which the personal
And political converge. I did not become more
Somber and mature as the years sped by

I did not write poems that were desperate
Bewildered or astonished. I did not plumb the depths
In search of a moral encounter with human principles

I did nothing to revive poetic architectures
I did not take pains to ensure my poems performed
Against a backdrop of political, social and ethical values

I did not write a book in which themes and images
Resurface, satisfying the reader who, by now, has become
Increasingly anxious and is in need of comfort

I did not write my poems in either a plain or high style
I did not try to motivate the reader to tears or action
My writing is not considered remarkable for its spiritual force

My poems do not travel across a landscape of cultural memory
They do not strike a dynamic balance of honesty,
Emotion, intellectual depth, and otherworldly resonance

They will not startle you out of your daily anesthesia
They do not map the deepest crevices of the interior self
They cast no light on history's margins, overlooked and neglected

Nor is it sacrilegious to comment on my poems
What they lack, their absence of resonant wit,
What they fail to fulfill, worlds they miss out on

Acknowledgements

Poems have been published in *Poetry*, *Volt*, *BOMB*, *Boston Review*, *Hambone*, *Prelude*, *Jubilat*, *Fruta*, *The Café Review*, *The Brooklyn Rail*, *Hotel*, *The Guardian* (England), *Normal* (Spain), *Poem-a-Day* (Academy of American Poets), *PoetryNow* (a partnership between the Poetry Foundation and the WFMT Radio Network), and *Lyrikline* (Haus für Poesie). My thanks to the editors.

"At The Tomb of Narcissus" was commissioned by ACE Gallery on the occasion of an exhibition by Alexander Yulish.

Egyptian Sonnets was published as a chapbook by Rain Taxi in 2012.

Black Threads from Meng Chiao was published by TIS Books in 2015, with photographs by Justine Kurland.

Midway was published as an artist's book by Gervais Jassaud under his imprint Collectif Génération in 2017. The artists who worked on separate editions were Kathy Barry, Claude Viallat, Chuck Webster, and Astrid Sylwan. My thanks to all of them.

Bijoux in the Dark is dedicated to Thomas Nozkowski.

I would like to thank the following individuals for their support. Anselm Berrigan, Joseph Donahue, Alan Gilbert, Andrew Joron, Enrique Juncosa, Amy King, Eugene Lim, Eric Lorberer, Albert Mobilio, Laura Mullen, Barry Schwabsky, Brandon Shimoda, Arthur Sze, Lisa Wells, and Joshua Marie Wilkinson.

John Yau is a poet, fiction writer, critic, editor, curator, and publisher of Black Square Editions, a small independent press that has published books and broadsides of poetry, fiction, criticism, and translation, as well as prints. He has contributed essays to many catalogues and museum publications, as well as written for *Art in America*, *Artforum*, *Art News*, *New York Times*, *Los Angeles Times* and *Art Press*. His work is included in many anthologies of poetry, fiction, and criticism, and has been translated into French, German, Italian, Portuguese, Spanish, and Chinese.

After serving as the longtime Arts Editor for the *Brooklyn Rail* (2007-2011), he left and helped start the online journal *Hyperallergic Weekend,* where he frequently posts his reviews.

He has received awards and fellowships from the John Simon Guggenheim Memorial Foundation, National Endowment of the Arts, Academy of American Poets, New York Foundation of the Arts, Ingram Merrill Foundation, and the General Electric Foundation. He has been named a Chevalier in the Order of Arts and Letters by the French government.

He is Professor of Critical Studies at Mason Gross School of the Arts (Rutgers University) and lives in New York.

Letter Machine Editions

Renee Angle, *WoO*
Cristiana Baik & Andy Fitch, editors, *The Letter Machine Book of Interviews*
Anselm Berrigan, *To Hell With Sleep*
Edmund Berrigan, *Can It!*
Peter Gizzi, *Ode: Salute to the New York School*
Aaron Kunin, *Grace Period: Notebooks, 1998-2007*
Juliana Leslie, *More Radiant Signal*
Farid Matuk, *This Isa Nice Neighborhood*
Fred Moten, *the feel trio*
Fred Moten, *The Service Porch*
Sawako Nakayasu, *Texture Notes*
Travis Nichols, *Iowa*
Alice Notley, *Benediction*
Andrea Rexilius, *Half of What They Carried Flew Away*
Andrea Rexilius, *New Organism: Essais*
Brendan Shimoda, *Evening Oracle*
Sara Veglahn, *Another Random Heart*
John Yau, *Bijoux in the Dark*
John Yau, *Exhibits*